A FAMILY ACTIVITY BOOK

Puppets and Marionettes

WRITTEN AND ILLUSTRATED BY

ROGER LEWIS

NEW YORK: ALFRED·A·KNOPF

THIS IS A BORZOI BOOK,
PUBLISHED BY ALFRED A. KNOPF, INC.

L. C. catalog card number: 51-13020

Copyright, 1952 by Alfred A. Knopf, Inc. All rights reserved. No part of this book may be reproduced in any form without permission in writing from the publisher, except by a reviewer who may quote brief passages and reproduce not more than three illustrations in a review to be printed in a magazine or newspaper. Manufactured in the United States of America.
Distributed in Canada by Random House of Canada, Limited, Toronto.

Contents

Introduction

PUPPETS

POTATO PUPPET	2
HOLLOW PUPPET HEAD	4
PAINTING	10
MAKING HAIR	12
MORE PUPPET IDEAS	14
HANDS	16
BODY	20
COSTUME TIPS	22
STAGES	24

MARIONETTES

HOLLOW MARIONETTE HEAD	26
SOLID MARIONETTE HEAD	28
BODY	30
LEGS	32
ARMS	34
CONTROLS	36
CONTROL STICK	38
STRINGING	40
COSTUME	42
ACTION	44

Introduction

The art of puppetry is ancient and honorable. Every civilization seems to have had puppets; children and adults have enjoyed them for thousands of years.

Here is a chance for you to make and operate your own puppet and marionette characters. The difference between the two is simple: puppets are operated by hand, while marionettes are controlled by means of strings.

Anyone can make these fascinating little creatures. You don't need a workshop or lots of tools. Any table will do for a workbench, so get busy right away!

Don't be surprised if your whole family becomes interested, for these "little people" appeal to everyone, regardless of age. Dad may be stringing a marionette, while Mother costumes another one.

Any doorway in your home is quickly transformed into a puppet theatre, and the show is on! You can produce your favorite plays and stories, or write your own. The sky is the limit, for you are in show business!

Puppets

POTATO PUPPET

You can use a potato to make a simple hand puppet. All you need is a large handkerchief, or a piece of cloth about 15 inches square. Select a potato with a lumpy surface. Using an apple corer or a thin bladed knife, make a hole in it about 2 inches deep; this is for your forefinger.

Now, using one of the potato's lumps as a nose, design the rest of the face. Make eyes by sticking in two thumb tacks, or use buttons, held in place with straight pins. Draw the mouth with lipstick. Use eyebrow pencil to draw the eyebrows.

Make hair by cutting pieces of wool yarn into ½-inch lengths, then gluing them all over the head. If you like, you may cover the head with a cap, instead. Simply cut the toe from an old stocking or sock, roll up the cut edges, and pin it to the head.

Drape the handkerchief over your hand. Use rubber bands to fasten it to the fingers that work the puppet. Push your forefinger into the hole in the potato, and the puppet is finished. Remember, vegetable puppet heads last only a few days.

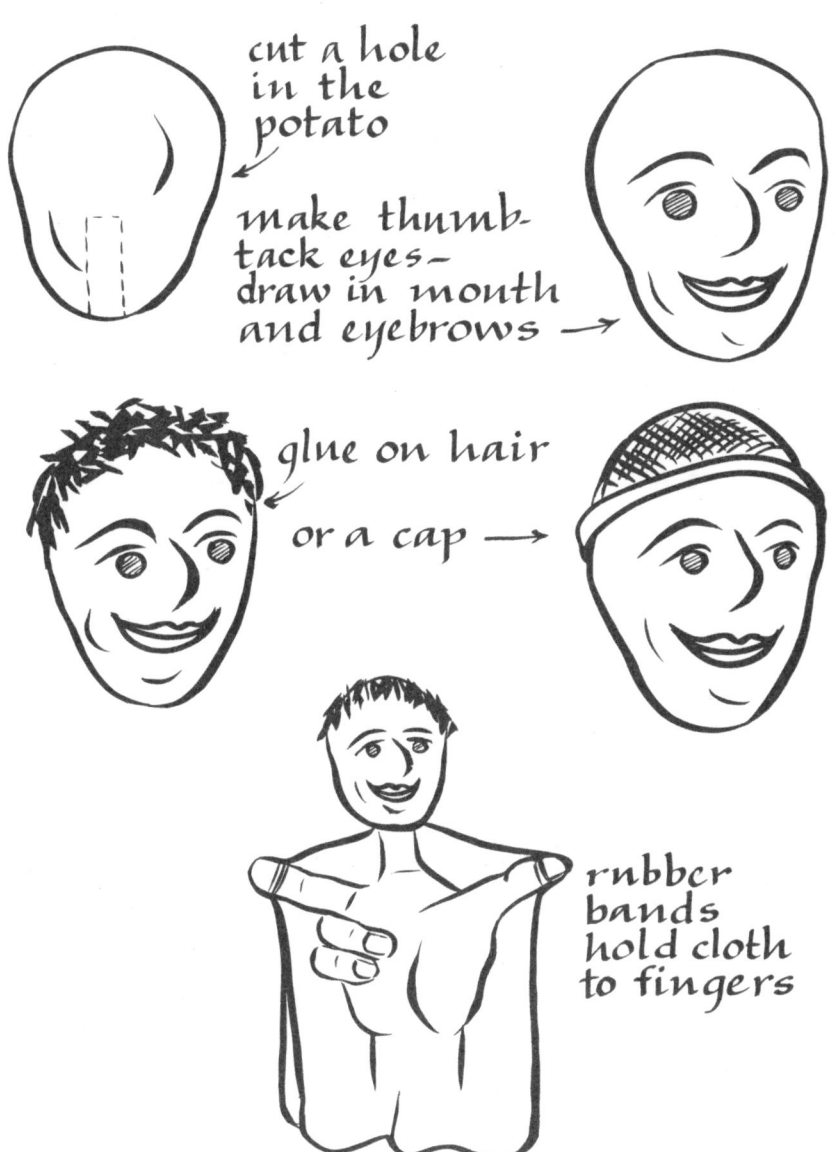

HOLLOW PUPPET HEAD

This hollow, papier-mâché (pronounced: paper ma*shay*) head is light in weight, and very strong.

Drive a large nail into a piece of wood about 4 inches square. This makes a stand upon which you can model the puppet head in clay.

Use 1 pound of plastalene (non-hardening clay), and shape it upon the nail, so that it looks like an egg with a long, tapering neck. Don't use all the clay; save some for the features. Make eye sockets by pressing your thumbs into the clay. Add pieces for the nose, chin, and ears. You don't have to shape a mouth, as that may be painted on. Don't model the hair; it will be added later, after the papier-mâché cast has been made.

Now, using your finger, smooth all the pieces you have added, blending them into the egg-shaped head. Shape the bottom of the neck so that it is slightly flared. The finished head should be about 5 inches high, and 3 inches wide.

Make all the features large, so that they can be seen clearly from a distance.

Papier-mâché can now be applied to the head.

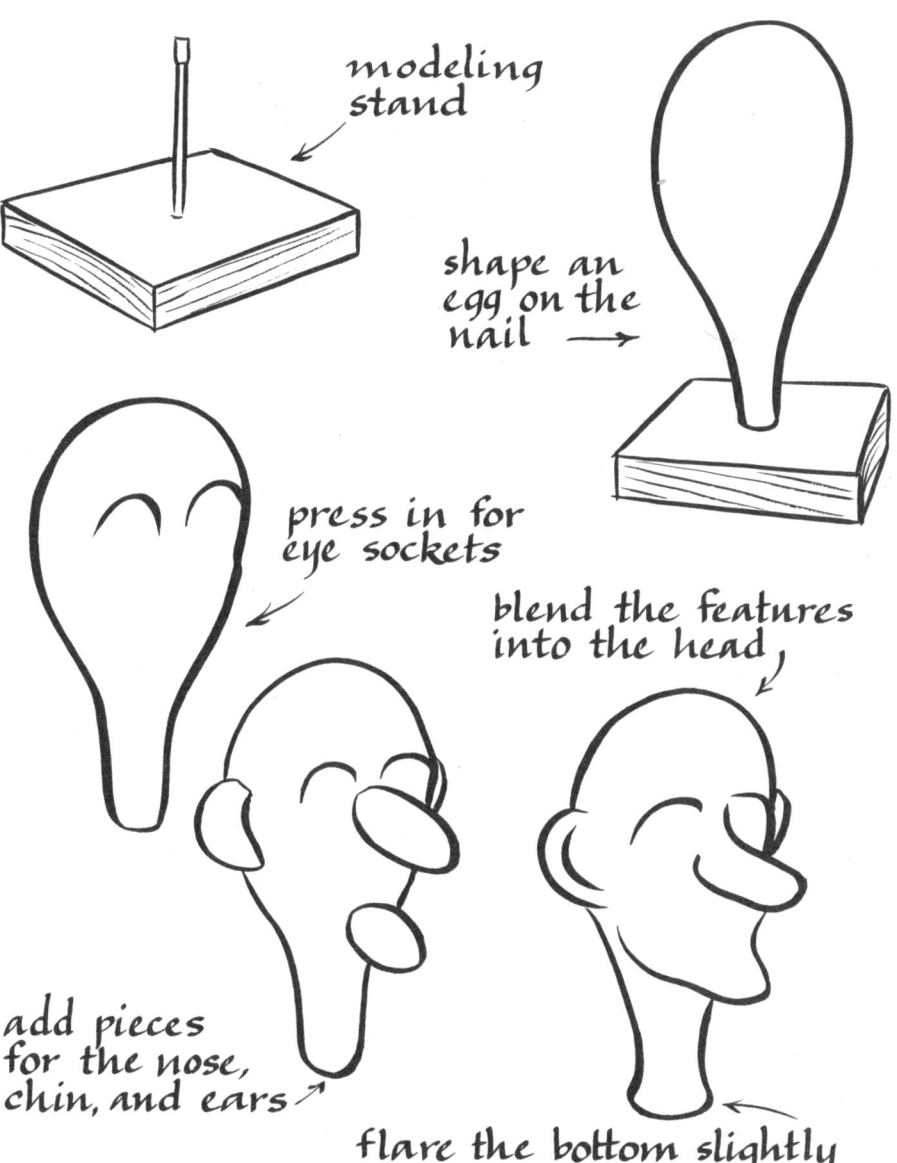

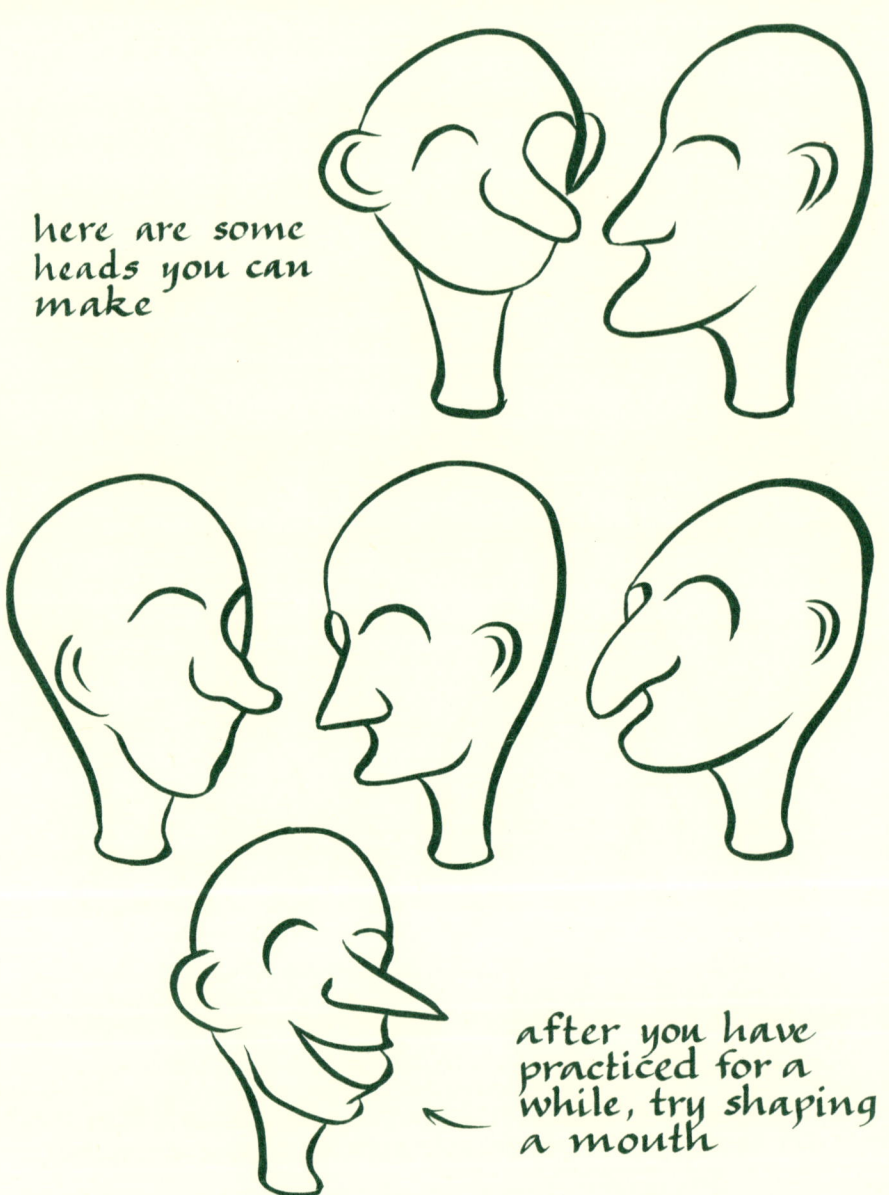

here are some heads you can make

after you have practiced for a while, try shaping a mouth

HOLLOW PUPPET HEAD, *(continued)*

In order to work with papier-mâché, you must have paste.

Almost any white paste is good for papier-mâché work. Use any of the following:

Library paste is thick, white paste that comes in tubes or jars. Dilute the paste with water, until it is thin and creamy.

Paper-hanger's paste may be bought in powdered form, in 1-pound packages. Fill a jar half-full of water. To this, add half as much paste powder as you have water. Stir it, making a thick paste. Allow it to stand for about ten minutes; the paste will thicken. Mix more water with the paste, until it is thin enough to be poured. Add a few drops of oil of peppermint or oil of wintergreen to give it a pleasant odor, and prevent it from spoiling.

Flour paste is made by adding enough water to ½ cup of flour to make a thin, creamy mixture. Boil this over a slow fire for about five minutes, stirring it constantly. This thickens the paste. Allow it to cool, then stir in cold water until it is again thin and creamy. Add oil of peppermint or oil of wintergreen.

Keep paste mixtures in covered jars, so that they do not dry.

HOLLOW PUPPET HEAD, *(continued)*

Tear (do not cut), newspaper into strips about ½-inch wide, and 2 inches long.

Dip a piece of torn paper into thin paste solution. Apply it to the clay head, smoothing it down so that there is no space between the paper and the clay. Apply another pasted strip, crossing it over the first. Keep pasting down strips of paper, crisscrossing them, until the entire clay head has been covered.

Now, using a *different* kind of paper, apply another layer of torn strips in the same manner. You may use paper towelling, or colored comic sheet paper. This makes it easy for you to tell when you have applied a complete layer. Apply five layers of paper, alternating the two kinds you are using. Allow the head to dry hard.

Cut through the paper shell along the sides and top of the head. Remove the two paper halves from the clay. (When making papier-mâché casts ask an older person to cut them apart for you. Papier-mâché is very hard; a slip of the knife may cause an accident. Let's be safe, not sorry.) Fit the edges together, then apply crisscrossed pasted strips over the joined edges. Allow the head to dry, and it is ready for painting.

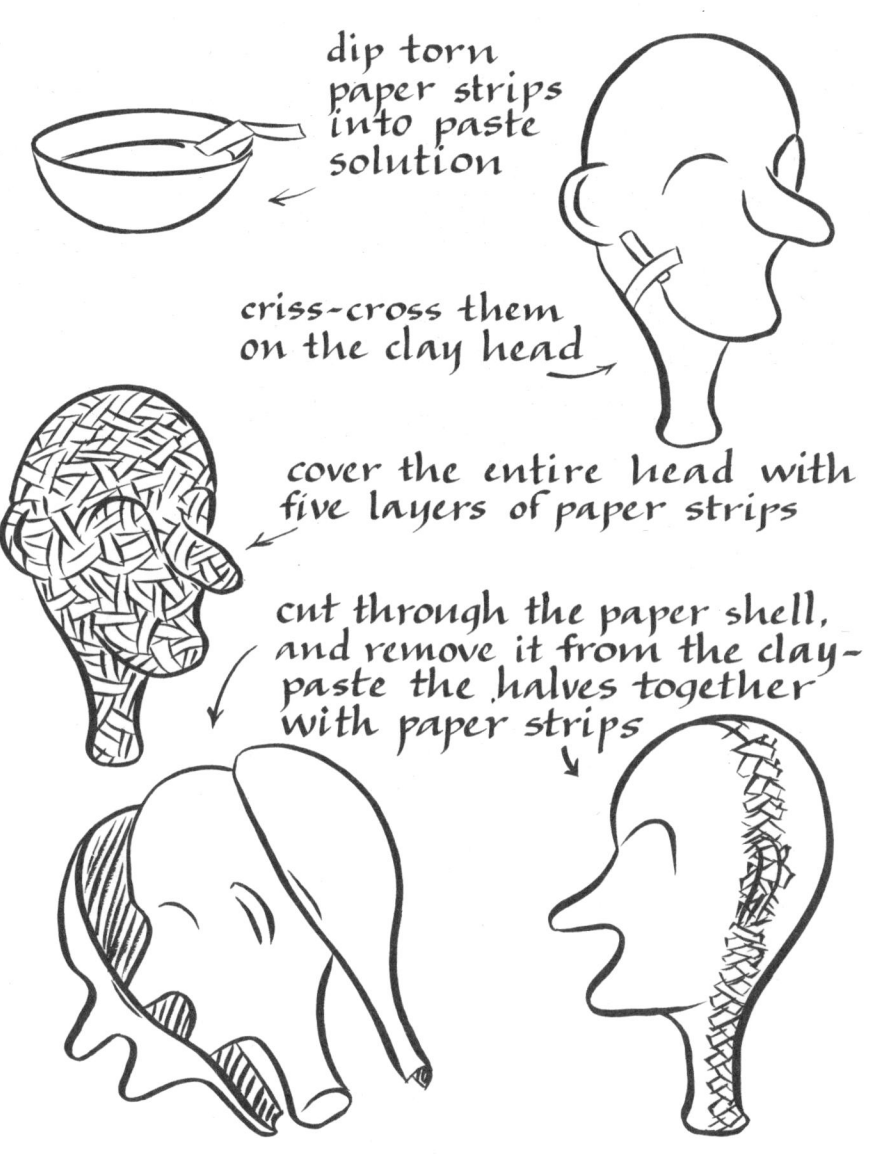

HOLLOW PUPPET HEAD, *(continued)*

Painting the head

Use tempera (show card) colors; these come in tubes or jars. To make flesh color, add a little red and yellow to white. Thin the color with water so that it can be brushed easily. Paint the entire head. While it is still wet, blend a little red into the tip of the nose, the cheeks, and the point of the chin.

Outline the shape of the eyes lightly with pencil. Paint the entire eye white. When this is dry, paint a large blue circle in the center of each eye. After the blue has dried, paint a slightly smaller black circle inside the blue, to make the pupil of the eye. Now, outline the eye with a soft pencil.

Paint the lips red, and outline the eyebrows with black.

When all the tempera paint has dried thoroughly, give the head a coat of shellac. Allow the shellac to dry, and you are ready to apply the hair. Shellac can be applied easily by using an insecticide sprayer.

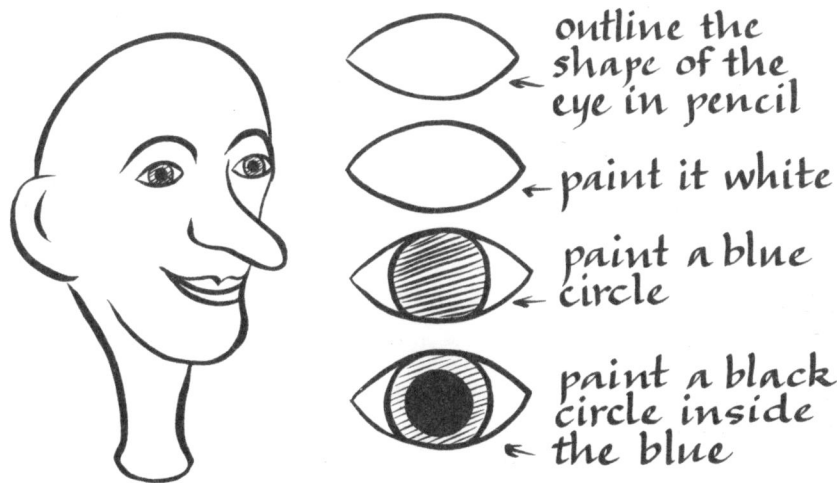

outline the shape of the eye in pencil

paint it white

paint a blue circle

paint a black circle inside the blue

paint the lips red, then divide the upper and lower lips with a pencil line

eyebrows should be thinner at the ends —

— unless you are making someone fierce — then you make them thicker near the nose

HOLLOW PUPPET HEAD, *(continued)*

Making hair

The simplest hair style to make is a crew cut. Use scissors to cut wool yarn into tiny shreds. Using model airplane cement, coat the head where the hair is to be, then pat the shredded wool over it. Use lots of cement.

Longer wool strands are used to make many different types of hair for girls and women. First glue on pieces that extend over the front of the head, and down the back. Then, glue long pieces crosswise over these, running from side to side. You may cut the hair short all around, or make bangs in the front, and braids at the sides.

For soft, silky hair, use strands of embroidery silk, then comb out the ends so that they are fluffy.

Use colored yarn—black or brown for brunettes, yellow for blondes, and red for redheads.

Try other materials for hair. Bits of fur can be glued on and trimmed with a pair of scissors. Ordinary steel wool makes excellent gray hair.

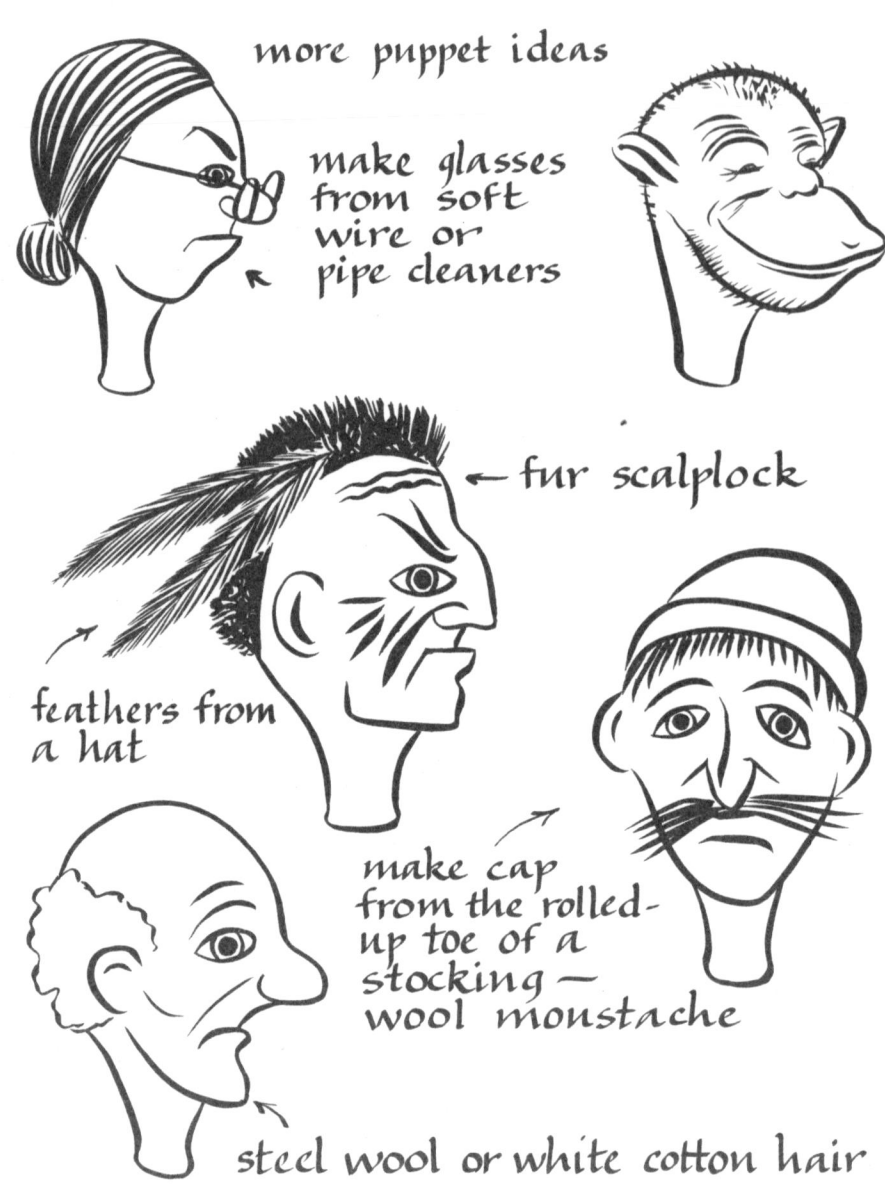

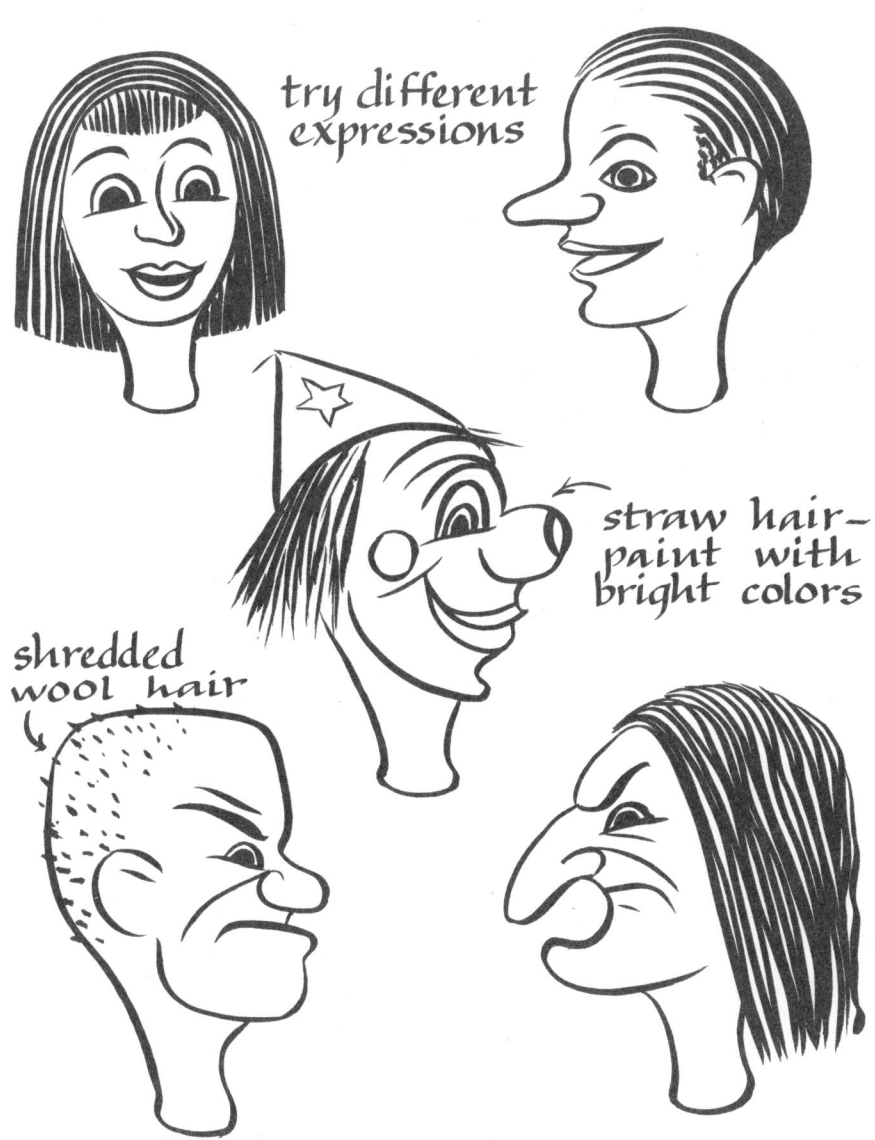

PUPPET HANDS

Cut 2 pieces of thin cardboard 2 inches wide and 6 inches long. Roll these into tubes; one should fit your thumb, and the other, your middle finger. Paste down the ends of each roll, or fasten them with a strip of cellulose tape.

Cut two pieces of soft iron or copper wire 8 inches long. With your fingers, shape these like mittens. Bind the mittens to the cardboard tubes with sewing thread, or a strip of cellulose tape.

Cut adhesive tape into strips about ¼-inch wide and 3 inches long. Wrap the tape strips around the wire mittens. With a few other strips, fasten the mittens to the tubes.

Bend the thumb of each taped mitten toward the palm, then bend the palm slightly inward. Make a right hand, and a left hand.

Now, crisscross pasted papier-mâché strips over both mittens and tubes. Apply the strips until hand appears smooth. Allow the hands to dry, then paint them with the same flesh color you used for the puppet head. Give them a coat of shellac, and the hands are finished.

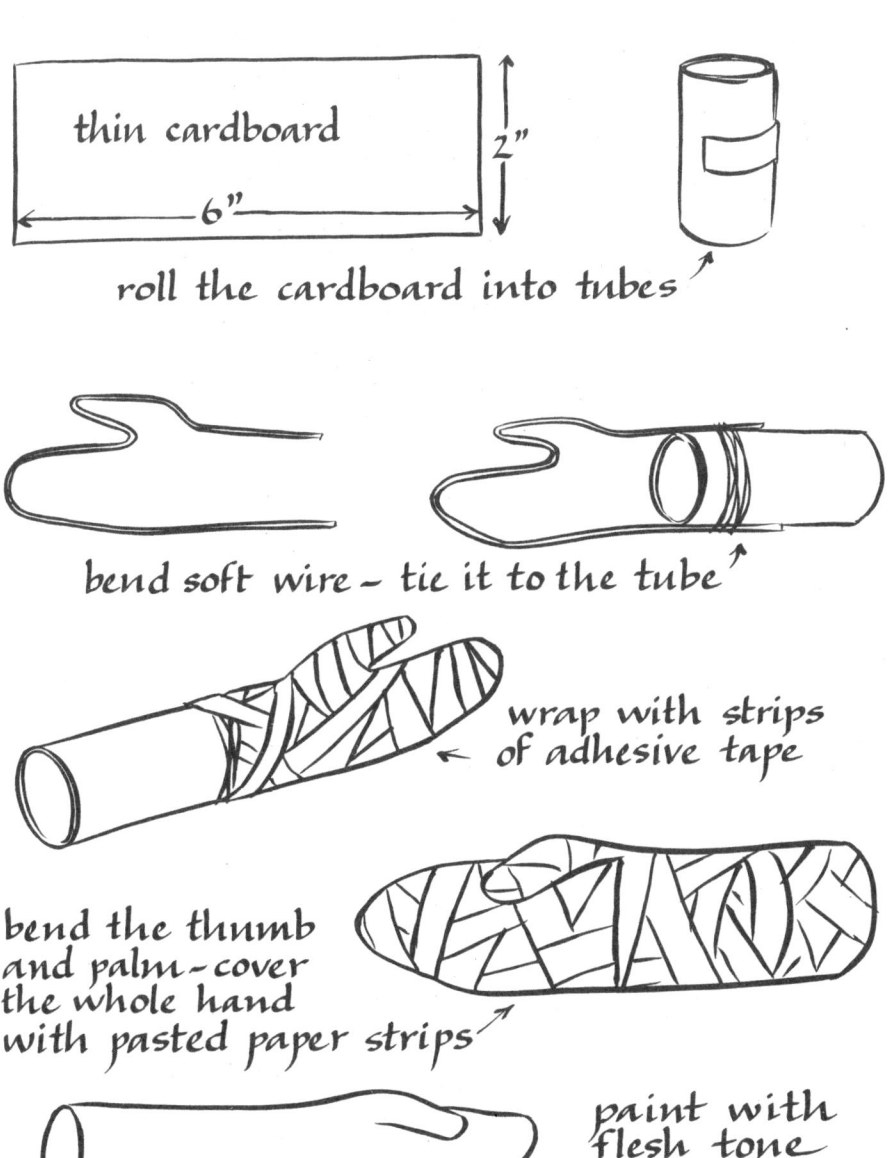

PUPPET HANDS, *(continued)*

There are other ways to make puppet hands. Choose the method that is easiest for you.

Felt: For each hand, cut two felt mittens, exactly the same size. Stitch them together to stiffen them. These hands will later be sewed into the hand openings in the body.

Papier-mâché: Model the hands in plastalene. Cover them with four layers of papier-mâché strips, then allow them to dry. Cut the hands in half, remove the plastalene, then fasten the two paper shells together with criss-crossed strips, exactly as you did the head. Finish the hands by painting them with flesh tone, then shellacking them.

Carved: Use balsa wood, or soft pine. Carve the hands with a sharp knife, then sandpaper them. Finish the hands by painting them with flesh tone, then shellacking them.

Be careful! Unless you are an experienced carver, don't make wooden hands.

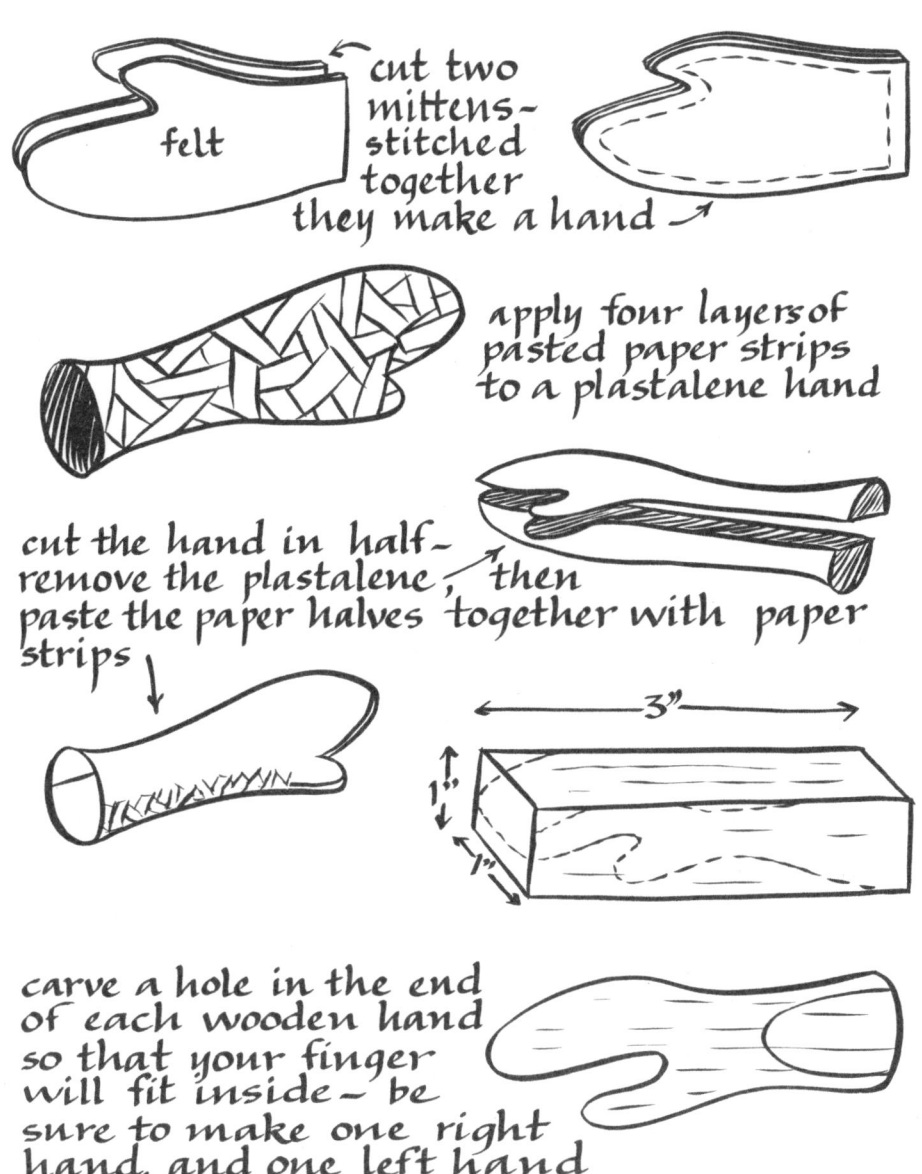

PUPPET BODY

Copy the body pattern on a piece of paper or thin cardboard. Cut it out. Place the pattern over a piece of cloth, and mark around it with a piece of chalk. Cut out the cloth with a pair of scissors. Mark and cut 2 pieces.

Place the pieces of cloth together, wrong sides out. Pin them together along the edges, and sew seams where shown in the drawing. Turn up and sew the bottom, too.

Put your finished puppet head *inside* the body, face up, and fit the neck into the neck opening. Apply a little model airplane cement to the lower part of the neck, then tie the cloth around it by wrapping it with five or six turns of cord.

Place the hands inside the body, push the tube ends into the hand openings, and tie them loosely *without* gluing them. Turn the body right side out, and check the positions of the hands. Be sure the right and left hands are in their proper places. Change their positions if necessary, by simply turning them within the sleeve.

Turn the body inside out, then cement and tie the hands as you did the head.

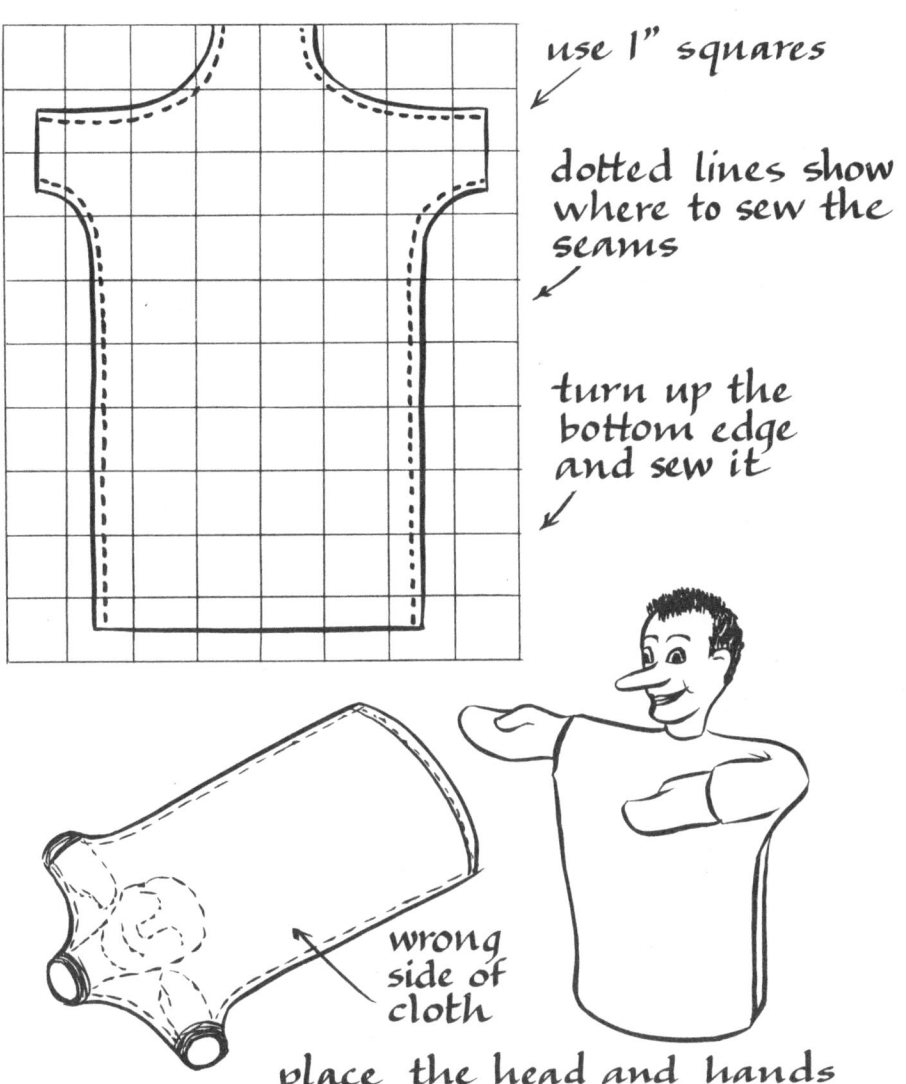

use 1" squares

dotted lines show where to sew the seams

turn up the bottom edge and sew it

wrong side of cloth

place the head and hands inside the body, then cement and tie them

costume tips for female puppets

← hair ribbon

shape collar like this →

← cuffs →

sew on buttons

make belt from a scrap of oilcloth or leather

← upholstery trimming

sew another piece of cloth over the body to make a skirt of a different color

try using different kinds of upholstery trimmings, such as moss fringe, ball fringe, bouclé, etc. — before cutting any garments from cloth, first make them out of paper to be sure they fit

costume tips for male puppets

shape collar like this

sew 2 pieces of cloth together to make a tie

make the body of colored or figured cloth

a piece of painted dowel stick makes a good puppet cigar

you can make legs by stuffing cloth tubes with cotton — sew them to the body — under the belt — stuff black cloth to make shoes, and sew them to the pants

PUPPET STAGES

Once the puppets have been completed, you are ready to give a performance; for this, you will need a stage.

Almost anything can be used as a temporary puppet stage. The simplest is merely a table, which has been turned on its side. A folding bridge table is excellent for this purpose.

A cardboard carton makes a good puppet stage, too. Cut off the top of the carton, leaving the bottom and four sides. Trim the sides, so that they are about 12 inches high. Cut out the center part of the bottom, leaving a frame about 4 inches wide, all around the opening. Now place the carton on a table, and there's your stage. If you like, paint the carton inside and out, and string a simple curtain across the opening.

Draping a cloth across a doorway creates another simple stage. First stretch a thin cord across the doorway; hold it in place with thumbtacks. Then, fold a sheet or other cloth over it. An old drape or bedspread will do nicely.

turn a table on its side and use it as a puppet stage

cut down a carton so that it is 12" high, then cut out the bottom — drape cloth around the table

drape a cloth across any doorway — operate puppets from behind — light up the front with reflector lamps, home movie and other lights — keep the back dark

Marionettes

HOLLOW MARIONETTE HEAD

Marionette heads may be hollow, or solid. One type of hollow head is made of papier-mâché, using the same method that is followed when making a hollow puppet head.

First, model the head in plastalene; be sure the bottom of the neck measures *exactly ½ inch across, and is perfectly round.*

Following directions given on page 8, build up five layers of papier-mâché strips. Allow the head to dry, then cut it in half. (Ask an older person to do this for you; sharp knives can be dangerous.)

Cut a piece of copper or iron wire, and place it between the paper halves, just above the ears. Fasten both halves of the head together, using crisscrossed paper strips. After the head has dried, use a pair of pliers to bend each wire into a tiny loop, to which strings will be tied.

Cut a piece of ½-inch dowel, 1 inch long. Round one end with a file or rasp; drive a ¼-inch screw eye into this end. Glue the dowel into the neck. When the glue has dried, the head may be painted. See page 10, for painting directions.

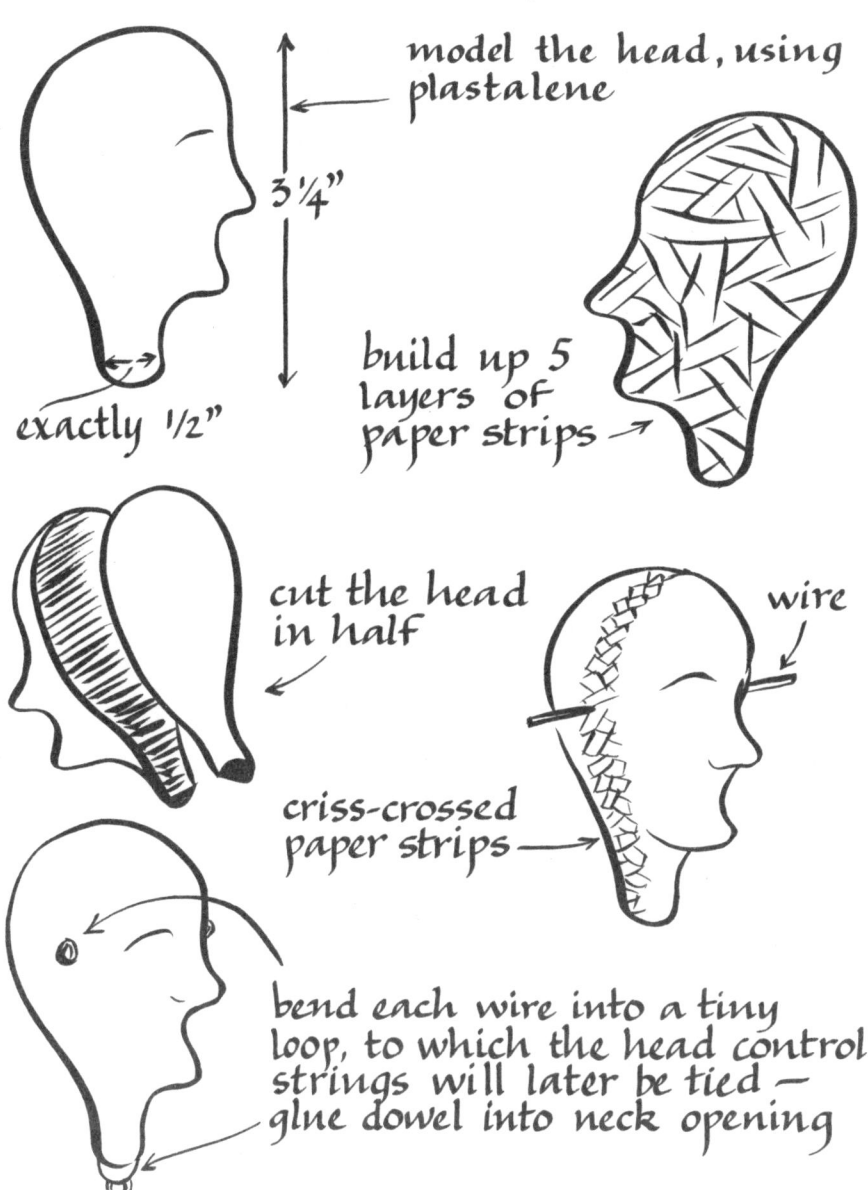

SOLID MARIONETTE HEAD

Pulp papier-mâché: Tear a sheet of newspaper into tiny pieces, and soak them overnight in hot water. Rub the wet newspaper through a kitchen grater, or a piece of wire window screening. Pour off as much water as you can, then remove the paper pulp and squeeze it between your hands until it is almost dry. Mix paste with the paper pulp, until it can be modelled like clay.

Use the pulp papier-mâché to form a head around a 3-inch piece of ½-inch dowel. Allow it to dry; this may take a day or two. Should the dowel loosen up, glue it back into place. Drive a ¼-inch screw eye into the bottom of the neck, then paint the head.

Carved wood: Use balsa wood, or other soft wood such as sugar pine or basswood. Draw a side view of the head upon the wood, then cut it out with a coping saw. Finish shaping the head with a wood rasp. Using plastic wood, add a nose, lips, and other details. (Keep your fingers wet, so that the plastic wood won't stick to them.) After the plastic wood has dried, sandpaper the head; then paint it.

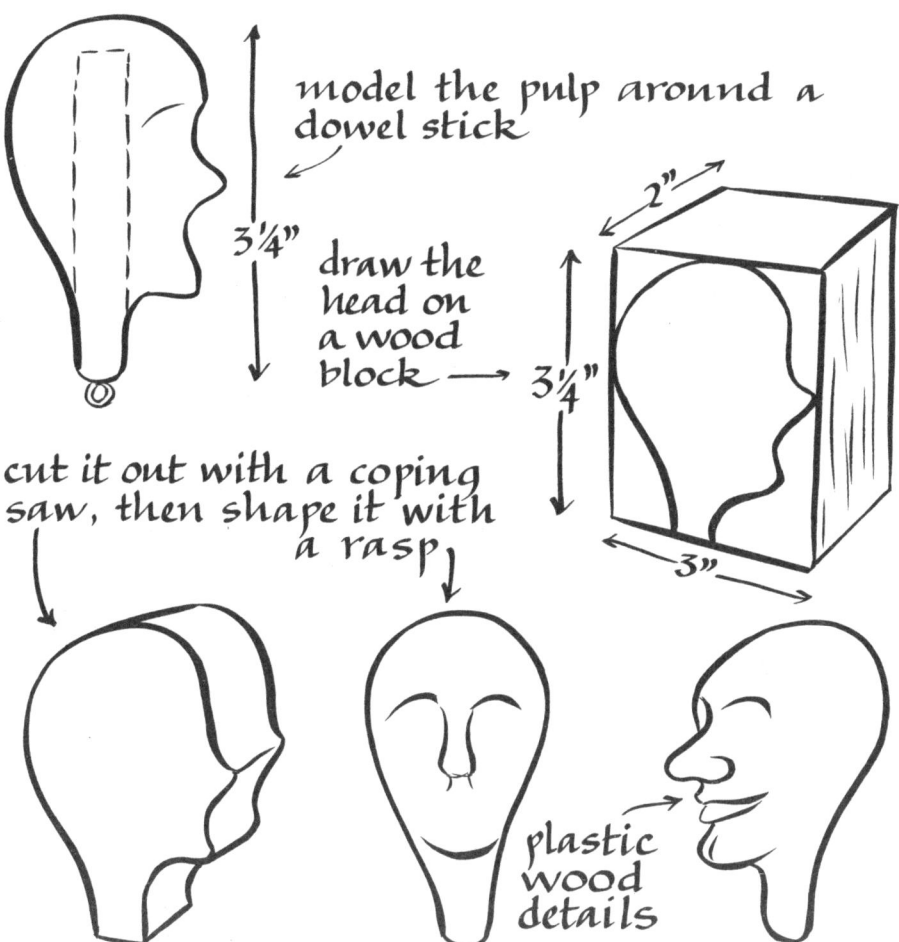

MARIONETTE BODY

Use ¾-inch wood; soft woods, such as white pine, sugar pine, and basswood, are best. A packing crate may furnish enough wood to make a dozen marionettes.

Draw the outline of each shape on a piece of thin cardboard. Cut out the cardboard shapes, then trace around them on a piece of wood.

Cut out each piece with a coping saw. Use a wood rasp to make the edges even, then sandpaper them.

Cut a piece of cloth 2 inches wide, and 7 inches long. Use any scrap cloth that is about the same thickness as muslin, percale, or sheeting. Wrap the cloth around the hips and the torso, forming a sash. Nail the cloth in place, using either #1 or #2 carpet tacks, or ⅜-inch wire nails.

Another way to connect the hip and torso is by using two screw eyes. Drive a screw eye into the center of the hip. Open a screw eye by twisting it with a pair of pliers, then drive it into the underside of the torso, directly opposite the screw eye in the hip. Link the two together, then close the open screw eye by squeezing it with a pair of pliers.

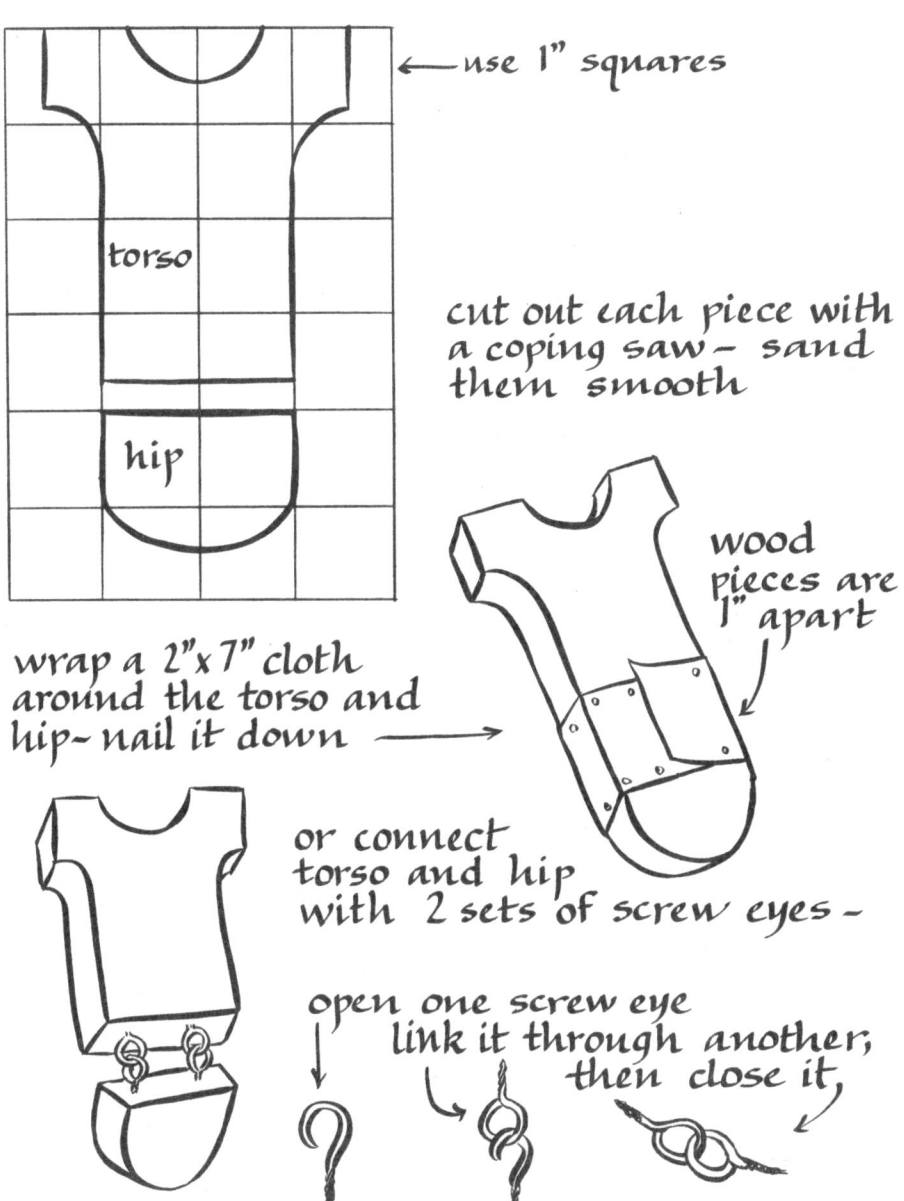

← use 1" squares

cut out each piece with a coping saw — sand them smooth

wood pieces are 1" apart

wrap a 2"x 7" cloth around the torso and hip — nail it down →

or connect torso and hip with 2 sets of screw eyes —

open one screw eye link it through another, then close it.

MARIONETTE LEGS

Use ½-inch dowel sticks. Cut a 3-inch piece for the upper leg, and a 3½-inch piece for the lower leg.

Draw the shoe outline on a piece of ¾-inch wood, then cut it out with a coping saw. Glue and nail the shoe to the end of the 3½-inch dowel; use a 1-inch wire brad. When the glue has dried, finish shaping the shoe with a wood rasp or file, and sandpaper.

Now make the knee joints. File a flat spot on each dowel, about ½ inch long, just behind where the knee would be. From an old purse or wallet, cut a strip of leather to fit this space, then glue and tie it to both leg pieces. Use sewing thread, adhesive tape, or cellulose tape.

Cut a piece of scrap cloth 2½ inches square. Fold it in half, then sew a seam down one side, ¼ inch from the edge. Turn it inside out, and you have a cloth tube, 2½ inches long.

Apply glue to the upper ½ inch of the leg, and slip the tube over it. Tie it securely with sewing thread. Tack the other end of the tube to the hip piece, as shown; use #2 carpet tacks, or ⅜-inch wire nails.

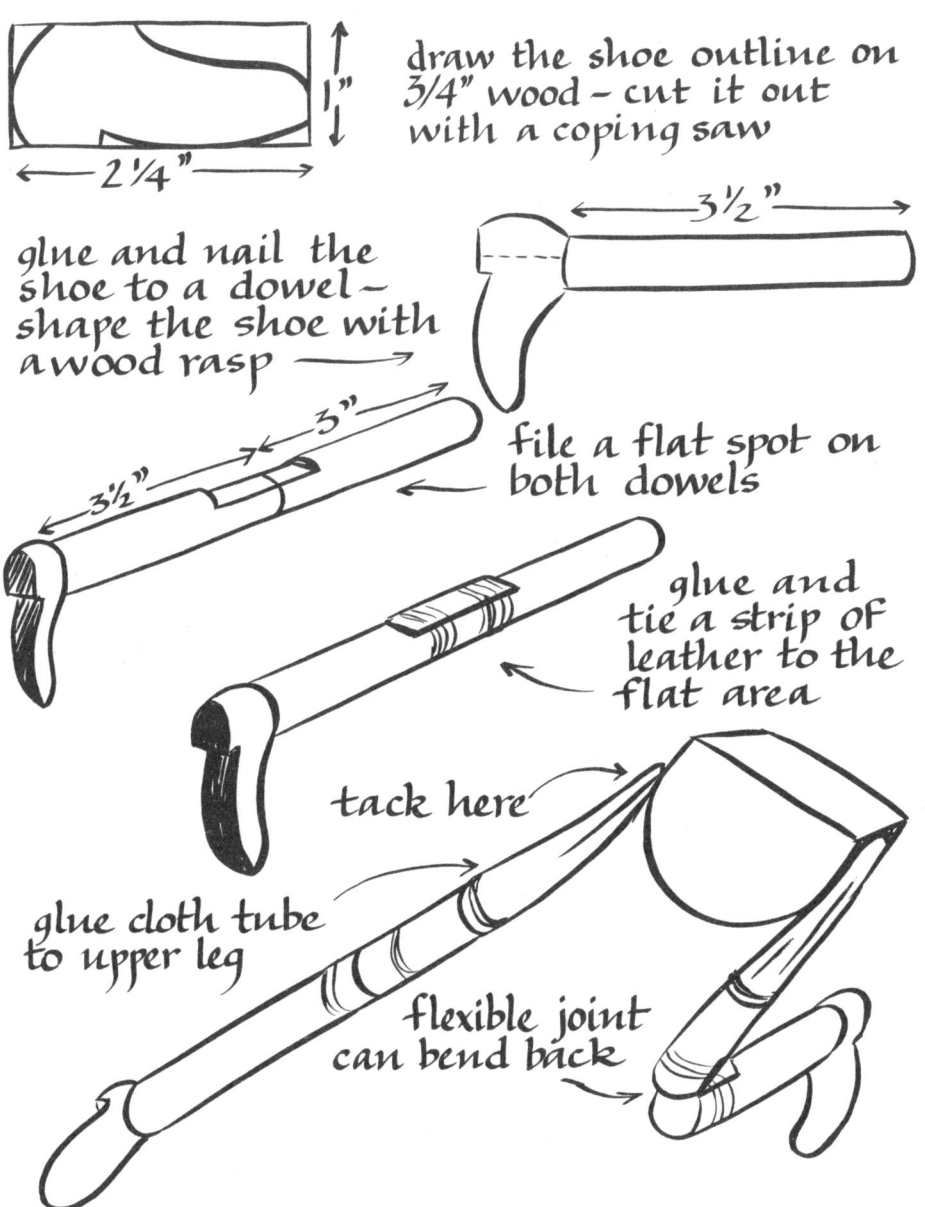

MARIONETTE ARMS

Use ½-inch dowel sticks. Cut a piece 2 inches long, for the upper arm.

Bend an 8½-inch piece of wire around the hand outline shown on the opposite page. The small loop behind the thumb is for a hand control string.

Strap the wire hand to the end of the 2-inch dowel; use adhesive tape or cellulose tape.

Cover the entire hand with papier-mâché strips, crisscrossing them halfway up the dowel, as well. Allow the hand to dry, then use a pair of scissors to trim the paper close to the wire form. You may leave the hand as it is, or build up its shape with plastic wood. Paint it with flesh tone.

Cut a piece of cloth 5 inches long, and 2½ inches wide. Fold it lengthwise, and sew a seam ¼ inch from the edge. Turn it inside out, making a cloth tube 5 inches long. Apply glue to the upper part of the arm, and slip the tube over it. Tie it securely with about ten turns of sewing thread. Put a little absorbent cotton into the upper part of the arm. Tack the other end of the tube to the top of the shoulder.

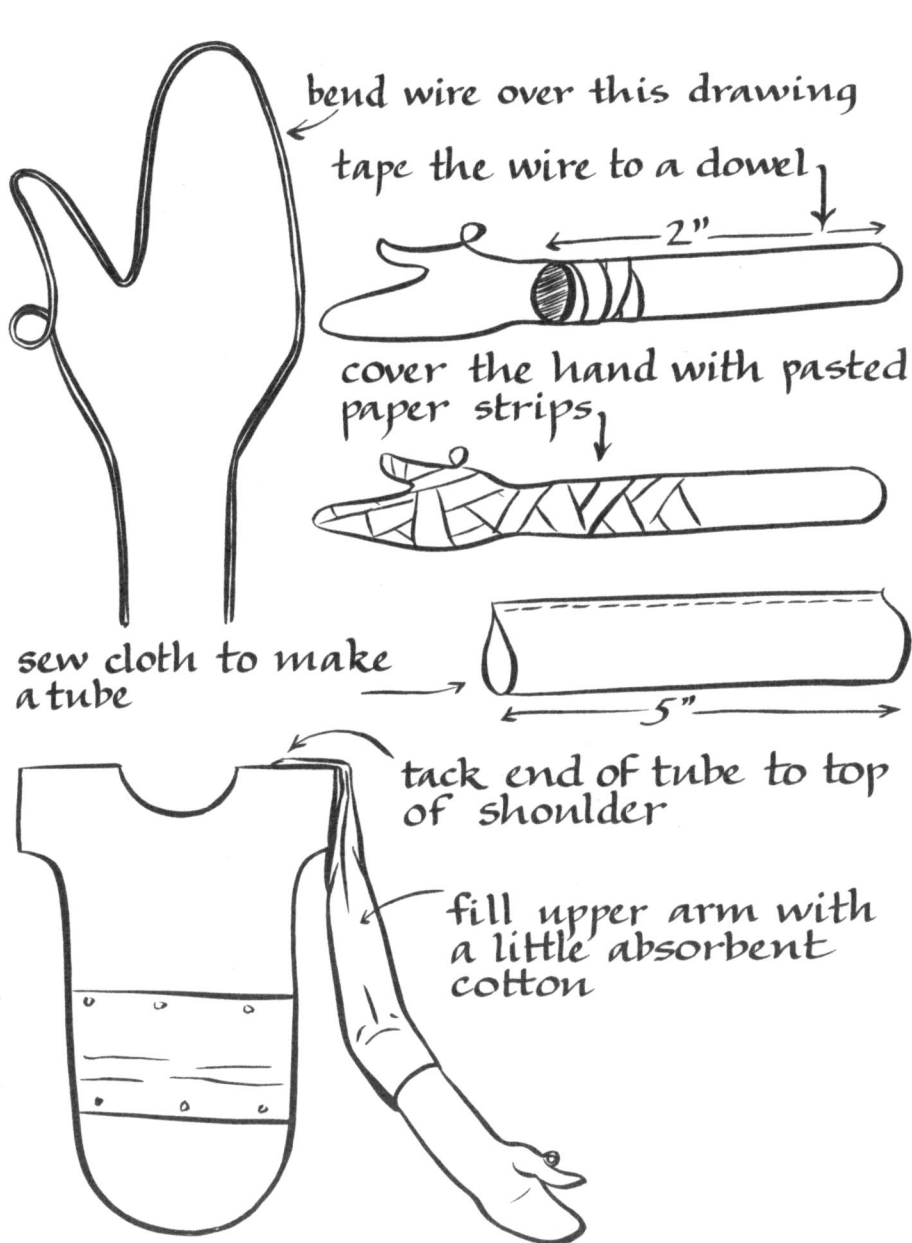

MARIONETTE CONTROLS

Drive a screw eye into the top of the torso, where the head is to be attached. Remove the screw eye, and open it. Hold one side of the loop portion with a pair of pliers, and twist the other side with another pair of pliers. Replace the screw eye.

Link the head to the open screw eye, but do not close it.

If you are using a hollow papier-mâché head, you have already provided wire loops for the head controls. If the head is made of pulp papier-mâché or wood, you must set in a screw eye just above each ear. These are the head controls.

Place screw eyes at the following points: one at the top of each shoulder; one near the bottom of the back of the torso; one at each knee.

Use a ¼-inch screw eye to hold the head in place. Those used for other parts of the marionette should be the smallest size obtainable—about ⅛ inch.

Now let's make the control stick, with which the marionette is put through its paces.

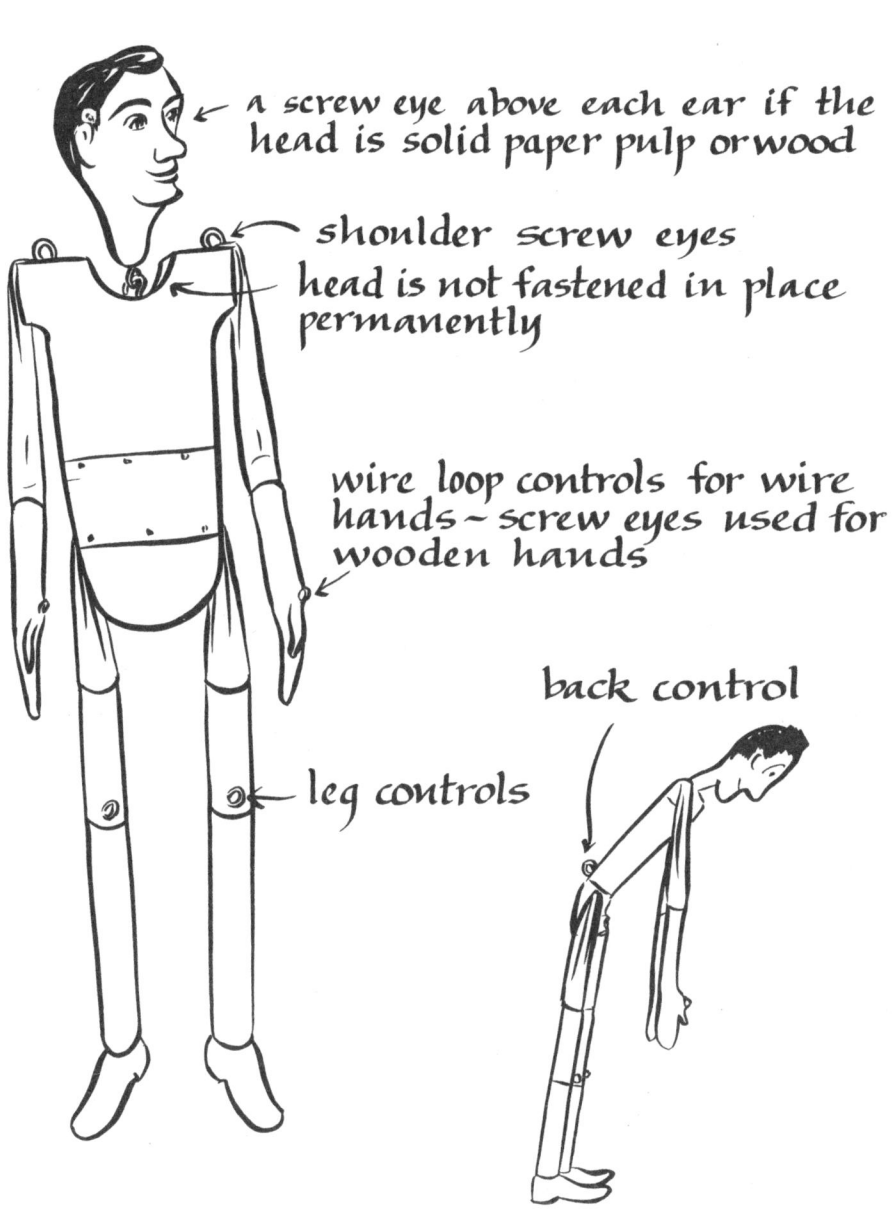

MARIONETTE CONTROL STICK

Use lattice wood, which is ¼ inch thick, and 1 inch wide. Cut a 6-inch piece, a 7-inch piece, and an 8-inch piece.

Glue and nail the 6-inch piece across the end of the 8-inch piece, as shown. Using a ¼-inch drill, bore a hole through both pieces. Cut a 1½-inch length of ¼-inch dowel; round one end with a file and sandpaper. Apply glue to the other end, and tap it into the hole you have drilled.

Drill a ¼-inch hole in the center of the 7-inch foot bar. Sandpaper the glued dowel in the control stick until the hole in the foot bar can be slipped over it without binding.

Insert a screw eye into each side of the control stick, 3 inches from the back end; these are for the shoulders. Insert two screw eyes into the front end of the control stick; these are for the hands.

With a coping saw, make three cuts about ¼ inch deep in the ends of the foot bar and the control stick. These will hold the ends of the strings that control the feet, the head, and back. Now, let's string the marionette.

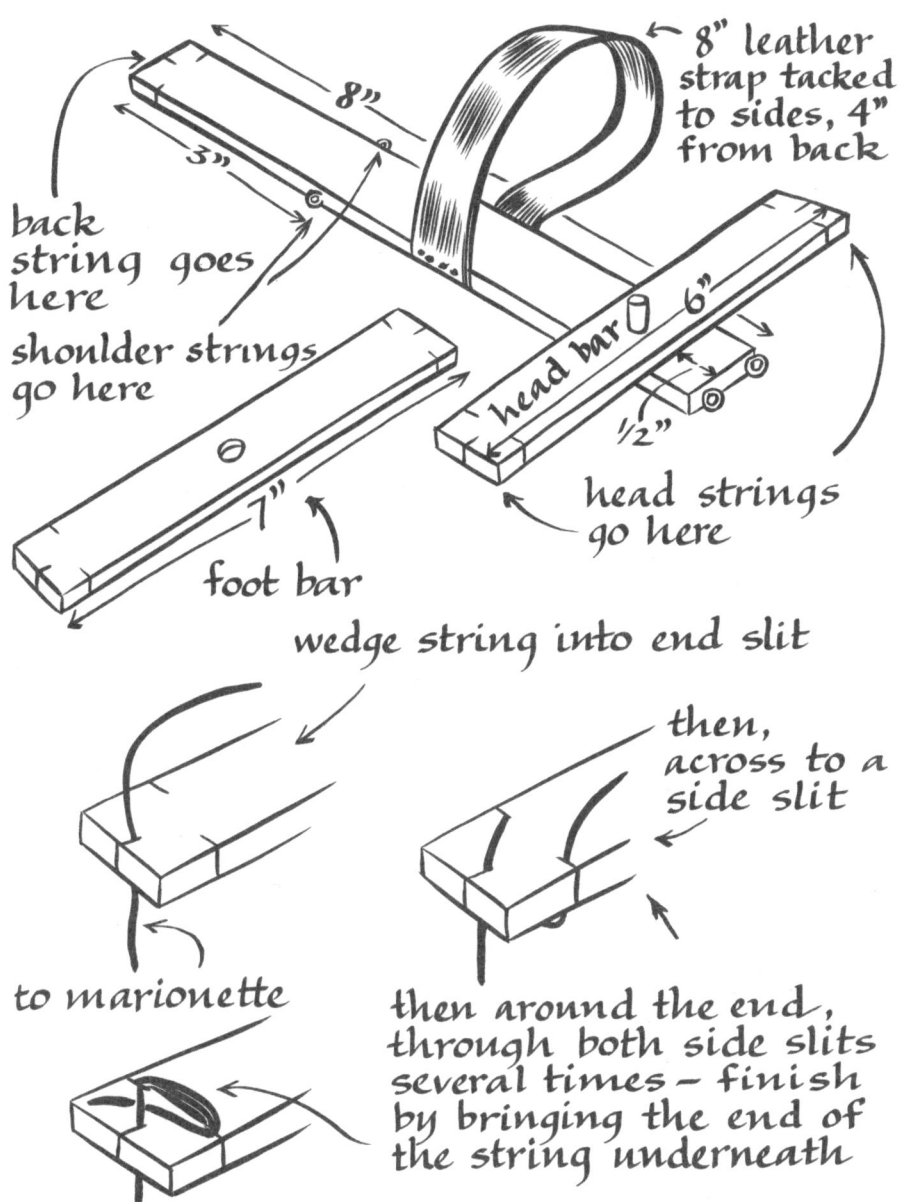

STRINGING THE MARIONETTE

Hang the control stick about 40 inches above your workbench or working surface. If you can't do this, slip a coat hanger over the top edge of a door, and suspend the control stick from it, 40 inches from the floor.

Use thin, black fishing line, or carpet warp thread for stringing. Suspend the marionette by its shoulders, so that its feet just touch the floor. Tie the strings to the shoulder screw eyes, then fasten them to the control stick screw eyes in such a way that they can be untied easily.

Tie strings to the head, and fasten them to the control stick as shown. Don't pull the head up tight; it should hang forward just a bit. String the knees to the foot bar; allow enough slack so that the foot bar can be lifted over the dowel without moving the legs. String the torso to the control stick; leave the line slack.

String a slack line from one hand, through both screw eyes, and tie it to the other hand. Don't tie the line to the control screw eyes.

The marionette may now be costumed.

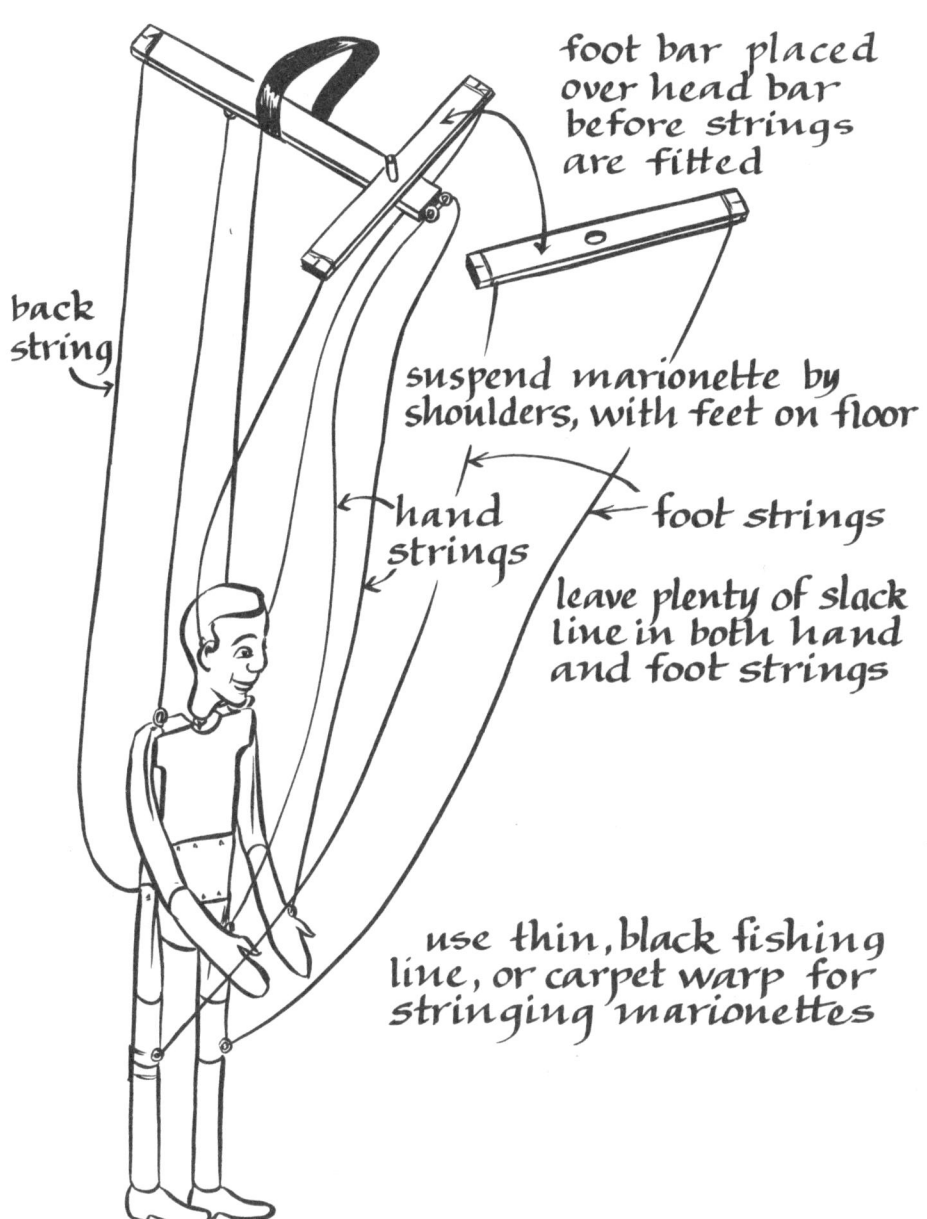

MARIONETTE COSTUME

Remove all lines from the control stick. Slip the head out of the open screw eye to which it is linked.

Make loose clothing, so that the marionette can move freely. Don't use stiff cloth.

Trousers: cut 2 pieces of cloth; fold each piece in half, wrong side out. Sew a seam ¼ inch from the edge; stop sewing 2 inches from the top. Place the two legs together, and continue to sew, joining both pieces. Turn the completed trousers inside out.

Shirt: fold the cloth in half, wrong side out. Sew a seam along the top and side; slit the sides 1 inch down from the top to make sleeve openings. Sew simple cloth tubes for sleeves. Sew one end of the tube to the cloth around the sleeve opening, placing the right sides of each piece together. Turn the shirt inside out.

Dress the marionette, then link the head back in place, and pinch the bottom screw eye closed with a pair of pliers. Thread the control strings through a large-eyed needle, and pass them through the clothes. Re-string the marionette on the control string.

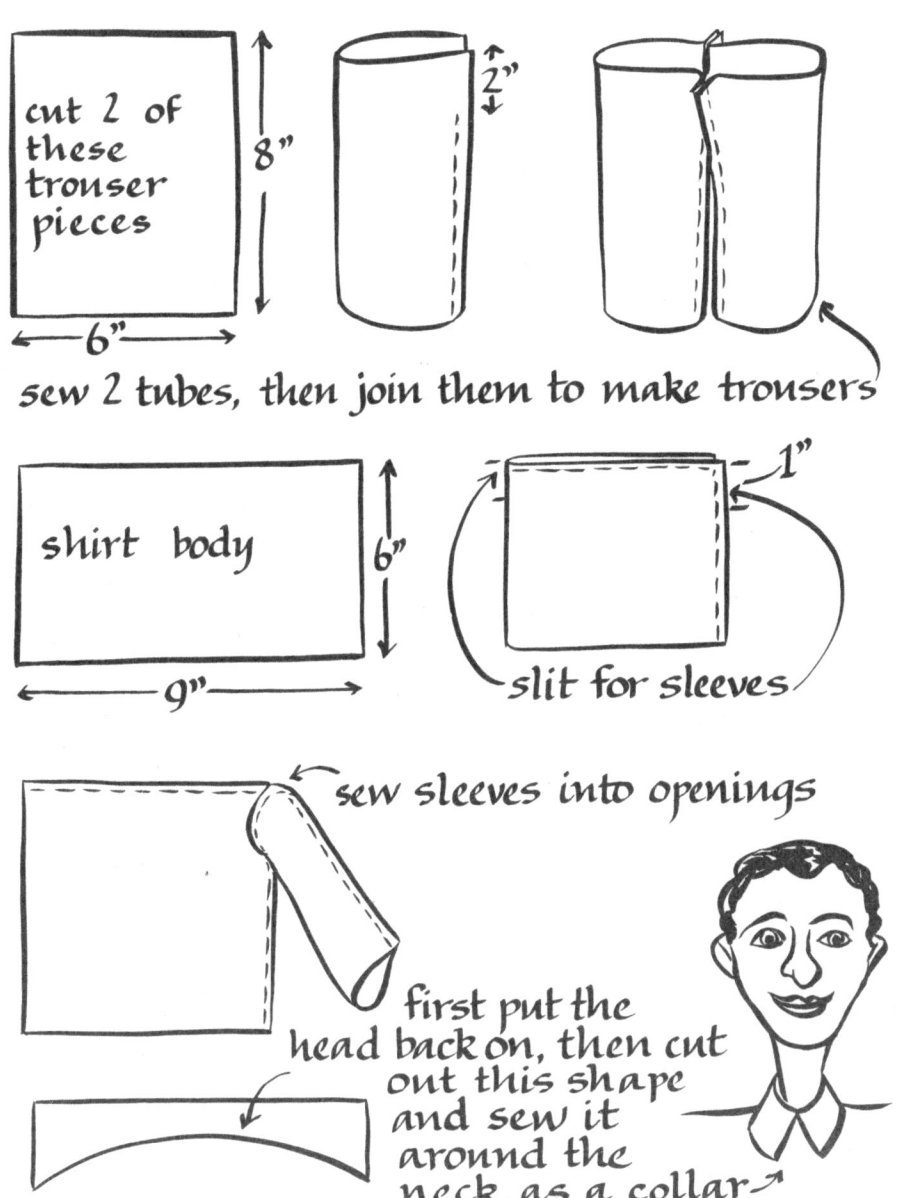

MARIONETTE ACTION

Hold the control stick in one hand, with your fingers between the shoulder strings and the head bar. Your other hand holds the foot bar.

Hand movements: Stand the marionette in a balanced, upright position. Reach over with the hand that holds the foot bar, and pull one or both of the hand strings. Practice slow, deliberate movements.

Walking: Raise one side of the foot bar at a time; this raises one leg at a time. At the same time, move the marionette forward with a very slight bouncing action.

drape a cloth behind a doorway
use a folding table or a large carton as a backdrop
tack up paper scenery
performer is hidden behind the backdrop

keep your marionette in a cotton drawstring bag between shows — hang it up by the strap on the control